SONG OF THE AUTUMN WIND

I SWEEP across the new-born day
  And set the red leaves flying;
Urge laggard swallows on their way,
  For summer dreams are dying.

I swing the sails of Wrawby Mill;
  The golden grain is pouring!
While high above the grassy hill
  I watch the kestrel soaring.

I shred and scatter every cloud
  And hush the brown lark's singing;
Send restless swans, so white and proud,
  To distant waters winging.

So sigh for Summer if you will,
  I yield to no such yearning.
All hail to Winter, stark and chill;
  May Spring be long returning!

Peter Cliffe

COUNTRY CHURCHYARD, POLAND

ONCE, nightingales in summer sang,
    and evening bells from belfry rang,
and lilacs nodded clustered heads,
and flustered dames with eager tread
bustled through the cobbled street,
and old men hobbled out to meet
their friends for Evensong.
There were lilacs everywhere,
scented, sweet upon the air,
and nightingales in Summer sang
in perfumed trees while church
bells rang, for Evensong.

And is it still the same today
when villagers set out to pray,
the nightingale so proudly sing,
the church bells loudly, roundly,
ring, the lilac toss its clustered
head above the cross of those long
dead,
At Evensong?

Agnes Kordylewska

EVENING

IN the dusk of a summer's evening
  Little things move in the hedge,
And only the black of the mountains
Holds back the round world's edge;
The loch seems self-illumined,
Eve's very soul is still,
And a star seems too much movement
Like the plover's warbling trill.

The smell of sea-tangle rises
To mix with the meadow-sweet,
And the cattle are crouched in the bracken
After the shimmering heat;
The songbirds roost in silence
And among the grasses lush
The spirit of night is gliding
Whispering "Hush" and "Hush".

Wendy Wood

YELLOW-AND-BLUE

YELLOW-and-Blue
  Sat on my bed
And nodded the curls
  Of her yellow head.
Her blue eyes danced,
  Her cheeks were red,
Her little pink hands
  Expressively spread.
Words tumbling over
  Each other, she said,
" Yellow crocus is up
  Out of his brown bed,
The scillas are blue
  Near the garden shed,
The Spring has come
  And the Winter is dead,
Oh, you ought to be out,
  And you're here instead!"

Sweet Yellow-and-Blue
  Sat on my bed,
The sun in my room
  Was her shining head.
" My Spring is you,
  Little Yellow-and-Blue,"
Was all that I said.

                    Mabel V. Irvine

THE INVITATION

LEAVE the town behind you
    And come you west away,
Where Cranham woods, deep-folded,
Make coolness all the day.
Green roof of high-arched branches,
Dim aisles of columned shade,
Soft floor of russet beech-leaves
Thick-drifted down the glade.

Come away to westward,
And leave the town behind,
The breath of Cranham woodlands
Comes blowing down the wind;
The scent of white wood-roses,
(Sweet tangled drifts of bloom),
Of honey-fragrant woodbine,
And green things in the gloom.

Leave the town behind you
And come you to the west,
The wind through Cranham woodlands
Shall sing your heart to rest.
Oh! Leave the glare and turmoil,
The sands that never cease,
The hush of Cranham woodlands
Shall steep your soul in peace.

Eva Dobell

THE VOICES

MY folly it was made my home within sound of
the sea,
Within sight, within reach of the beach and the
boats in the lee;
That built of its shingle and sand the four walls of
my home,
Within sound of the call of the wind, within sight of
the foam.
And now I must choose, I must choose — and none
knows what that choice is —
Yet I win not, nor lose; I am won by the lure of their
voices;
The strong, irresistible call of the wind and the sea,
And the deep, the ineffable peace that is she, that is
she.
And if I must go, you will know 'tis no wish for the
going
That draws me afar by the light of yon pilot star
glowing.
And if I go not, you will know that my old love is
sleeping,
Or my heart is gone cold. I am old, then, and ripe
for the reaping.

Malcolm K. MacMillan

THE WEE GREEN ROADS

IT used to be, when I was wee,
    With places to go and things to see,
My mother was always telling me
Of the wee green roads of Ireland.

I know the Seven Hills of Rome,
The Isle where Venus left the foam,
But still my thoughts keep turning home
To the wee green roads of Ireland.

I'll buy a horse at Dublin Show
And one fine morn away we'll go
With a clatter of hoofs and a "Cheerio!"
For the wee green roads of Ireland.

With satin nose and velvet eye,
And ears aprick to the morning sky,
He'll send the milestones skipping by
Down the wee green roads of Ireland.

We'll gallop round by Killakee,
His shining shoulder under my knee,
For that's the way that a man should be
On the wee green roads of Ireland!

There's many a place I'd like to be,
In France or Spain or Germanie:
But, oh my heart, I'd rather see
The wee green roads of Ireland!

Sydney Bell

SORROWS OF WERTHER

WERTHER had a love for Charlotte
    Such as words could never utter;
Would you know how first he met her?
    She was cutting bread-and-butter.

Charlotte was a married lady,
    And a moral man was Werther,
And, for all the wealth of Indies,
    Would do nothing for to hurt her.

So he sighed and pined and ogled,
    And his passion boiled and bubbled,
Till he blew his silly brains out,
    And no more was by it troubled.

Charlotte, having seen his body
    Borne before her on a shutter,
Like a well-conducted person,
    Went on cutting bread-and-butter.

William Makepeace Thackeray

THE WIND AND THE LARK

THE wind sang songs to the cherry tree,
  The lark soared high in the sky,
And I said to myself "What an indolent soul,
What an indolent soul am I,
Let me, therefore, work till the setting sun,
As the wind and the lark on their task begun."

For the wind moves always at God's behest,
And the lark will never arise,
To meet the dawn with a rapturous song,
All thrilling with sweet surprise,
Unless His messages first be heard,
By this sweet, obedient little bird.

So the wind caresses the cherry tree,
And the lark sings high in the sky,
And I say to myself "What a fortunate soul,
What a fortunate soul am I,
For I have a task of my own to do,
Like the wind and the lark my whole life through.
If I kneel in the morning awhile to pray,
I know I'll be guided as well as they."

Margaret H. Dixon

NEW YEAR

THE year's first day.
   Outside the upstairs window
the oak branch bounces;
Sun falls in floodlight
On the fields,
Throws hills in misty shadow,
Makes a high rise of winter trees
Bristle on the skyline.
A hint of sparkle
Leaps from the silver river . . .
And in the mile-off village
The church tower stands,
Anchored, inscrutable,
While late chimneys,
One by one,
Burst into life.

Margaret Gillies Brown

TREE IN WINTER

OLD tree, the snowqueen passed thee in the night
    And thrilled thee with the magic of her hand;
For now at dawn thy trembling arms rise white
    Above a world new-turned to fairyland.

The gleaming fretwork of the frosted leaves
    Stretches a silver web from bough to bough;
Bright threads the snow-sprite's shining shuttle
      weaves,
    White-hung by fairy fingers high and low.

Perchance, bowed down beneath thy load of snow,
    Unconscious of thy beauty, thou hast dreams
Of Summer, and hast sighed for winds that blow
    More softly and the song of sunlit streams.

Old friend, thou would'st not sigh could'st thou but
      guess
    That to one heart at least thy beauty now
Hath brought more joy of perfect loveliness
    Than e'er it did in Summer's golden glow.

Perchance when thou hast kissed the lips of Spring,
    And in thine arms the blossom slowly swells
To sunlit life, some hidden thought may bring
    A far off memory in thy heart that dwells:—
And mingled with the thrush's song shall ring
    The clear cold music of the Christmas bells.

Herbert Kennedy

MIDSUMMER MEADOW

HOME was a cottage near Midsummer
  Meadow,
    Beside an old bridge arching over a stream.
Bright were the flowers in my mother's front
    garden;
    Strong were my father's hands guiding his
    team.

Time had no meaning in Midsummer Meadow,
    Passing like clouds drifting over the hill,
Where in the cool, fitful breezes of morning,
    Turned the white sails of my grandfather's mill.

Life was a song out in Midsummer Meadow,
    Lilting and lingering, soothing and sweet.
The world was a plaything of sunlight and shadow,
    Small like the acorns I found at my feet.

Gone is my childhood in Midsummer Meadow,
    Ruined the cottage and silent the mill;
Ivied the stone arch above the swift water,
    But voices of loved ones are haunting me still.

                                    Peter Cliffe

LOVE'S SEASONS

IF you wish a sweetheart
  Seek her in the Spring;
Life is quick in bud and flower,
  Love is on the wing.

Through the long, bright Summer
  Wisely bide your time;
Lip shall meet with happy lip
  In Love's sweet rhyme.

Autumn ripens all things,
  Love will riper grow;
Arms around each other's waists
  Through the woods you go.

But Winter, chilly Winter:
  Tingling finger tips;
Even the very kisses
  Frozen on your lips;

That's no time for wooing;
  That's the time to make
A happy home, a snug fireside
  For Love's sweet sake.

Latimer McInnes

OUTWARD BOUND

MY heart is singing a merry lay,
  My pulses dance and thrill—
For the deck is under my feet once more
  And the bulging big sails fill,
As far astern the distant shore
  Sinks into the curving bay.

Give me the dip of the tall keen prow,
   The roll of the heaving poop,
And the slanting deck as the vessel heels
   To the wind's resounding whoop;
While the swinging foretop rocks and reels
   As through the billows we plough.

Steer me a course for the far south seas
   With the blue skies overhead,
Where the palm trees wave on enchanted isles
   That rise from the ocean bed,
And fetterless over a thousand miles
   Is wafted the scented breeze.

For there is never a lure for me
   In proud baronial halls,
Or titles, or land, or wealth untold,
   When the mystic ocean calls.
No gleaming gems or treasures of gold
   Can woo me away from the sea.

C. W. Wade

SUN AND SHADOW

OVER the meadow float the clouds,
　　And trail their shadows on the grass;
Shadows like ships with sails and shrouds,
　　Shadows like hills with peak and pass.

Lying beside the tinkling stream,
　　Watching the wind-swept shadows throng,
The changing shapes of clouds may seem
　　Anything if you look for long.

Pictures out of a fairy book;
　　Towers and battlements, marching crowds,
Dragons and all—how like they look!
　　Over the meadow float the clouds.

W. D. Cocker

JUNE MUSIC

ONLY the song of the leaves that sigh
    Of love to the lingering breeze,
Only the sob of a violin
Heard 'neath the dreaming trees.
Sweet as the sound of an angel's voice,
Sad as a sinner's sigh;
Exquisite pleasure, exquisite pain
Woke as it passed me by,
Woke and leapt and lived in my heart,
And faded not soon away,
But stayed as I lay with face to the sky
And watched the leaves at play.
Stayed to lighten the world and me
In the glare of the golden noon:
Sad as the song of the dead, yet sweet
As the first red rose in June.

Only the song of the leaves that sigh
Of love to the lingering breeze,
Only the sob of a violin
Heard 'neath the dreaming trees.
Yet half the joy in the world is born
Of memories such as these!

Herbert Kennedy

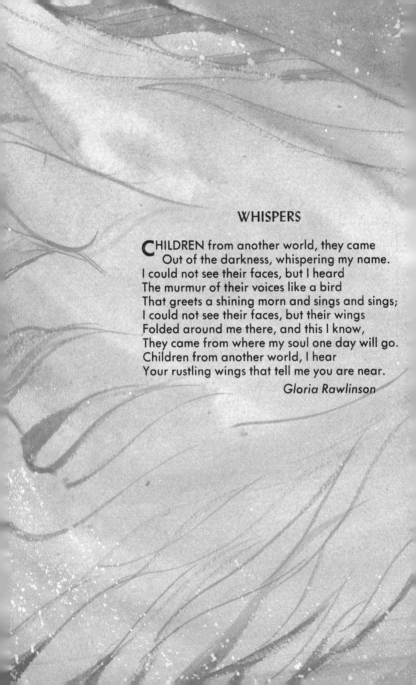

WHISPERS

CHILDREN from another world, they came
    Out of the darkness, whispering my name.
I could not see their faces, but I heard
The murmur of their voices like a bird
That greets a shining morn and sings and sings;
I could not see their faces, but their wings
Folded around me there, and this I know,
They came from where my soul one day will go.
Children from another world, I hear
Your rustling wings that tell me you are near.

Gloria Rawlinson

AUTUMN GARDEN

WHEN Autumn creeps with stealthy disarray,
   And frosts descend to melt flowers with their
     blight,
When Robin whistles that he means to stay,
And bright-eyed perches with no sign of fright
Upon the spade that's upright in the earth;
When flames of orange, red and gold, burn warm
Along the beech-hedge giving it new worth
Of gleaming splendour ere it turns, forlorn,
To working clothes of Cinderella brown;
When plum-tree stands dejected and alone,
Forgetting all the fruit that tumbled down
To fill the baskets we have proudly shown;
Then I remember all the bulbs that sleep,
And Spring will give me no more time to weep.

Arma Cochrane

THE BULLFINCH

A MOMENT on that twig he stood,
　　A bullfinch in the winter wood,
　　Alluring in his brightness.
'Mid russet leaves and tangled brake
And traceries of boughs there spake
　　His miracle's strange rightness.

From withered herb to branch's tip
He flew with rise and pause and dip,
　　A brilliant sturdy rover;
Fresh as the coloured image made
On some dark mediaeval page
　　For saint or courtly lover.

A brave thought in a dreary world
Where every devil's bolt is hurled,
　　A quickening of pulses,
Such joy it was to see his rare
Alighting here, delighting there,
　　Oblivious of repulses.

　　　　　　　　C. C. Abbott

ALL IN AN AUTUMN DAY

OH, I watched you in the morning,
    In your dainty gingham gown,
Choosing roses for our table,
    With a pensive little frown.

Then I saw you at the noonday,
    With a book upon your knee,
Lying dreaming in the hammock,
    Underneath the apple tree.

But best of all, this evening,
    As the mists begin to rise,
You are standing here beside me,
    With the moonlight in your eyes.

Peter Cliffe

MAIRI

No hand will lift the latch again
  At Mairi's door;
For it is barred to living men
  For evermore.

No voice will hail her cheerily
  Through the peat haze;
But echoes whispering eerily
  From other days.

Only the fingers of the wind
  Will tap at her pane;
And if anything stir, she will not mind:
  It is only the rain.

No smoke uprising from her roof
  A welcome sends.
Her house is quiet, cold, aloof,
  And she greets no friends.

No peat-stack stands with warm, brown mould
  For her winter fires.
Her hearth is long ago gone cold;
  She has no desires.

Long shall we seek ere we find again
  A heart like hers,
That slumbers deep in the quiet glen
  Of the whispering firs.

Malcolm K. MacMillan

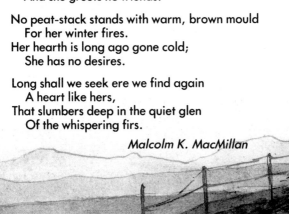

DOVER'S HILL

FROM this hill where the air's so clear
    We can see away and away,
And the villages, far as near,
Shine in the lucid day.
On rough short grass we tread
And thistles bend at our feet
And a lark sings overhead
And the clouds are white and fleet.
The wind is strong in our faces,
It drives us, we veer and yield,
And a broken thistle-top races
Over the tossing field;
But below, as we look around,
The deep long plains appear
Like a lost country drowned
In a tranquil flood of air,
Whence now and again there rises,
To the listener on this shore,
The muffled sound of the voices
Of bells that ring once more.

Edward Shanks

THE WAYFARER

SO many gardens I shall pass
   Before I find you, tired and late,
And maybe I shall cross the grass
   And linger at a gate,
Not yours — but you will wait.

So many miles are yet to run,
   You will not mind if I shall rest
An hour or so from rain or sun,
   And laugh awhile, and jest,
Some other's passing guest.

For you will keep your garden sweet,
  And yield its fragrance glad and free
To comfort those wayfaring feet
  That pass your gate ahead of me —
But only I shall keep the key . . .

Anne Page

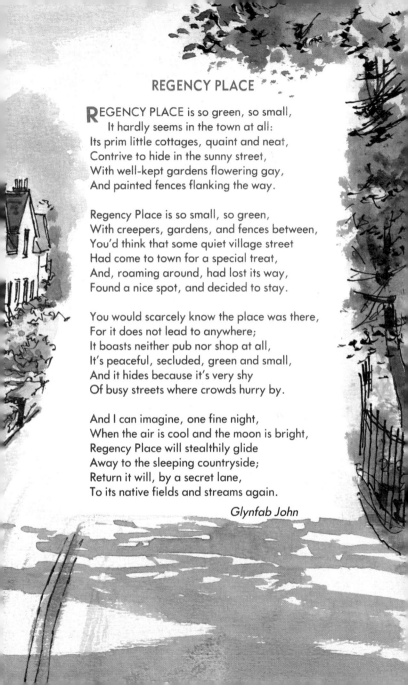

REGENCY PLACE

REGENCY PLACE is so green, so small,
   It hardly seems in the town at all:
Its prim little cottages, quaint and neat,
Contrive to hide in the sunny street,
With well-kept gardens flowering gay,
And painted fences flanking the way.

Regency Place is so small, so green,
With creepers, gardens, and fences between,
You'd think that some quiet village street
Had come to town for a special treat,
And, roaming around, had lost its way,
Found a nice spot, and decided to stay.

You would scarcely know the place was there,
For it does not lead to anywhere;
It boasts neither pub nor shop at all,
It's peaceful, secluded, green and small,
And it hides because it's very shy
Of busy streets where crowds hurry by.

And I can imagine, one fine night,
When the air is cool and the moon is bright,
Regency Place will stealthily glide
Away to the sleeping countryside;
Return it will, by a secret lane,
To its native fields and streams again.

Glynfab John

LITTLE I ASK

I DO not ask for love, I only pray
 This: that of all the smiles that day by day
Make sweet thy face, one, only one, may be
A star to light my feet upon their way.
              One smile enough for me.

'Tis little that I ask. When thou art gone
My world will darken, and the sun that shone
Grow dim. Till then — where'er thou art, to be—
Still, still, unseen, unknown, to love thee on—
              Enough, enough for me.

                                        Herbert Kennedy

MINGARY

THE road now led through wilderness.
  We'd left the brilliant trees behind;
Across the rain-soaked moors we drove,
Watching the switchback trail unwind
Before us like some pale-backed snake,
Down to where earth and sea combined.

The moors were yellow-russet-gold,
The sky a slate-stone-quarry grey
That did not manage quite to take
The feel of sun and warmth away,
Until we reached the great, grey sea
And the rock-bound shore at Mingary

Where fabled castle, dark and still,
Stood watching from the lonely bay
As shadowy islands came and went
In the fickle light of drowning day;
Where waves rolled slowly and slowly in
And time lost meaning at Mingary.

Margaret Gillies Brown

NIGHTFALL

THE sun retired in majesty,
    And flung a cloak across the sea
Of turquoise, gold and cramoisy,
In sweet farewell.

A glamour faded in the west,
All creatures of the day sought rest,
And there was peace within my breast,
As deep night fell.

Somewhere beyond the headland stark,
Where rolled the waves, white-tipped and dark,
I heard the warning sailors mark:
A solemn bell.

A harvest moon climbed o'er the hill,
A bird of night began to trill,
But why such magic haunts me still—
Ah, who can tell?

Peter Cliffe

SPRING PASSES

DEAD winter lies in the silken shroud
   Of the southwind, soft as a cloud,
And Spring strides over the moor today,
Lilting on his way.

He rests awhile in a sun-filled hollow,
Then calls the burns to follow,
They, all song and bubbling laughter,
Foam-flecked, hurry after.

Spring is out on his adventure
To do and to endure,
So he laughs when the fir trees creak and sigh
And stretch hands warningly.

His laughter floats the wide moor o'er,
And old things stiff and sore
Move again, while a glad desire
Sets young blood afire.

The whaup with a desolate, lost-soul cry,
Wails as he leapeth by,
And the peewit shrills to her harsh-voiced lover
That Spring is passing over.

Hylda C. Cole

TO AMARYLLIS

OH who would be, oh who would be
   A shepherd boy in Arcady?
Clear piping where the hilltops dream
And lightly laughs the mountain stream,
Or stretched along the gleaming grass
To watch the grey cloud-shadows pass,
And not a care the livelong day
From dawn of gold to twilight grey.
Oh I would be, oh I would be
A shepherd boy in Arcady.

Oh who would be, oh who would be,
A shepherd maid in Arcady?
To tend the flocks and softy sing
By woodland waters wandering:
Or garlands weave of woodland flowers
To crown her in the moonlit hours,
When from the sleeping hills above
Dance feet that she had learnt to love.
Oh thou should'st be, oh thou should'st be
A shepherd maid in Arcady.

Herbert Kennedy

NOVEMBER DAYS

I LOVE the fitful gust that shakes
   The casement all the day,
And from the glossy elm-tree takes
   The faded leaves away,
Twirling them by the window pane
With thousand others down the lane.

I love to see the cottage smoke
   Curl upwards through the trees,
The pigeons nestled round the cote
   On November days like these;
The cock upon the dunghill crowing,
The mill sails on the heath a-going.

The feather from the raven's breast
   Falls on the stubble lea,
The acorns near the old crow's nest
   Drop pattering down the tree;
The grunting pigs, that wait for all,
Scramble and hurry where they fall.

John Clare

THE ROSE " OPHELIA "

SHE dwells in my garden, so dainty and sweet,
   And her perfume's not heady, but subtle and
      sweet.
While June, ever changeful, sends sunshine or rain,
She modestly blossoms again and again.

When   soft   morning   breezes   are   playful,
      perchance,
Ophelia, she curtseys and joins in the dance,
And the cares that beset me seem feeble and few,
When I see that she's wearing a diamond of dew.

An opus in pastels, as fair as her name,
With petals that glow like the heart of a flame,
I love her so dearly; I'm certain she knows,
Gentle Ophelia—my favourite rose!

Peter Cliffe

GIVE ME THE SEA

GIVE me the sea where the breeze blows free
    O'er a thousand leagues of foam,
And the white clouds shift as they slowly drift
    O'er the sky's great azure dome.

Give me the dip of a gallant ship
    As she runs before the wind,
While the long waves churn as they roll astern,
    And the white wake trails behind.

Give me the spread of the sails o'erhead,
    And the graceful towering mast,
And the petrels' scream as they drift abeam
    Like leaves in the wintry blast.

Give me the gleam of the warm sunbeam,
    And the wide horizon's sweep,
Till day is done and the setting sun
    Sinks into the mighty deep.

Give me the night with its purple light,
    With the star dust overhead,
With the wide, wide sea to comfort me
    Till the last of life has fled.

Give me a day on the seagull's way,
    With the waves on every hand.
Give me the sea with its witchery,
    And I'll not ask for the land.

                                    C. W. Wade

THE OLD WOOD

O HAUNTS, old haunts, the haunts of boyhood's
     years,
  The mossed wood ways that woo loitering
    feet,
  The bird songs and the music low and sweet
Of falling waters sounding in my ears;
This leafy twilight-green that more endears
    Each ferny bank and sheltered nook replete
    With primrose, violet, and all things meet
For this dear April with her smiles and tears.

O woodlands solitude! how oft, how oft,
    When suns were hot and city pavements sore,
      And my parched heart was sick for sight of
      thee,
    Have I, a staring dreamer 'mid the roar
Of the vast tumult, heard thy murmurs soft
    And seen with inward eye what now I see.

Latimer McInnes

DAFFODILS

BLOW, blow your golden trumpets,
  Ye dancing daffodils!
Blow, blow your golden trumpets!
  For Spring has left the hills.

Low in the vale she lingers,
  And all her path along
The touch of her magic fingers
  Thrills all to life and song.

Pure at her breast there shineth
  The snowdrop's radiance fair;
The primrose her feet entwineth,
  The violet laughs in her hair.

The hawthorn buds are paling
  As snow-white flowers unfold;
The berberis is trailing
  Its glowing arms of gold.

The lily bells are ringing,
  The tulips burst apart,
And a nightingale is singing
  In the cherry blossom's heart.

O ring it out ye daffodils,
  Ye dainty, dancing daffodils;
O ring it out across the world
  That Spring has come again.

Herbert Kennedy

AUTUMN HOLIDAY

LET us take the road together
   In the sunny Autumn weather,
When the bloom is on the heather
And the hours drift by.

There'll be clouds like galleons sailing,
And a plover loudly wailing
For a golden Summer failing,
Now the short days fly.

Not a single task to bind us!
Leaving all our cares behind us
We shall roam where none can find us,
Where the brown streams flow.

And when stars above are gleaming
We'll forget our hopes and scheming,
While in blankets warm we're dreaming,
As the fire burns low.

Peter Cliffe

THE CURLEWS

N old friend spoke: " Last night
I heard the curlews cry
As they passed high overhead
In the loom of the sky,
Talking their way to the moors
Where memories lie."

And, said he, " When I was a boy
The curlews soothed my breast;
Last night, again, their cry
Brought quiet rest:
And in the silence that followed,
My sleep was blest."

" One thing I vow and declare "—
He smiled as he turned away—
" If from this life I go
To another world, some day,
And find no curlews there . . .
I shall not stay!"

Sydney Bell

LATE SNOW

IT'S almost April.
  The late snow falls
In soft white slants
And haze surrounds the river.
As though he hasn't noticed,
A blackbird sings and sings,
Spring calling from inside.
Each green-stick branch and twig
On the oak outside the window,
Is edged in frills of lace,
Shows up against grey sky.

This will not last.
Already, beyond the orchard,
Fir trees dip Christmas branches
To slip off furs of ermine,
Closer, snow thunders from the roof,
Roaring that Winter's not for ever.

Margaret Gillies Brown

ON YOUR BIRTHDAY

THE garden is cool at the close of day
   And the evening star is peeping.
Thrush and blackbird have flown away
   And the daisies all are sleeping.

The sunset gold has left the sky
   And the breeze is a sweet voice sighing.
All the butterflies have said goodbye
   And the first small bat is flying.

Then draw the curtains against the night,
   For your birthday now is ending.
The sandman has promised a dream so bright,
   Of love and happiness blending.

Peter Cliffe

THE WHIN-BUSH

THO' April was piping
    Young things to his dancing,
Half-shy they still waited
The glad tunes of May,
And dulled were my dreams;
In the grey world around me
No joy-lilt was ringing
No hope held a sway.

But sudden the greyness
Was pierced by a gladness,
A golden-hue'd riot
Of joy in gay bloom,
Where a whin-bush tossed bravely
Its sun-laden blossoms
And rang out a challenge
To dullness and gloom.

Like a cool tide-breeze banishing
Heat's weary languor,
Like the heart-warming look
When one, glad of you, nears,
Like a cheery word lifting,
A kindly thought soothing,
Is the glory of sunshine
A whin-bush uprears.

Hylda C. Cole

LOVE AND DEBT

THIS one request I make to Him that sits the
clouds above;
That I were freely out of debt, as I am out of love.
Then for to dance, to drink, and sing, I should be
very willing;
I should not owe one lass a kiss, nor ne'er a knave a
shilling.

'Tis only being in love and debt, that breaks us of
our rest;
And he that is quite out of both, of all the world is
blessed.
He sees the golden age, wherein all things were free
and common;
He eats, he drinks, he takes his rest, he fears no
man nor woman.

Sir John Suckling

SERENITY

ACROSS the fields the radiant sun
    Sinks slowly down to rest,
And softer, paler, dreamier hues
    Illuminate the west.
Now, like a drift of primroses,
    Or rosy-tinted snow
On misty hills of silver-green,
    The cloud-banks gently glow.
And listen — through the peaceful air,
    An owl hoots from afar,
And look — there trembles high above
    A tiny crystal star.
How lovely is the afterglow!
    One only hopes that we,
In our own sunset years will find
    Such sweet tranquillity.

Kathleen O'Farrell.

ACKNOWLEDGEMENTS

Our thanks to Margaret H. Dixon for "Glimpses of Spring" and "The Wind and the Lark"; to Peter Cliffe for "Song of an Autumn Wind", "Midsummer Meadow", "All On An Autumn Day", "Nightfall", "The Rose 'Ophelia' ", "Autumn Holiday" and "On Your Birthday"; to Agnes Kordylewska for "Country Churchyard"; to Margaret Gillies Brown for "New Year", "Mingary" and "Late Snow"; to Arma Cochrane for "Autumn Garden"; to Glynfab John for "Regency Place"; to Sydney Bell for "The Wee Green Roads" and "The Curlews".